USBORNE

Picture Atlas of
GREAT BRITAIN
and IRELAND

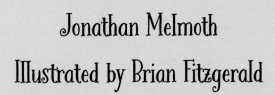

Jonathan Melmoth

Illustrated by Brian Fitzgerald

Designed by Samantha Barrett

Cartographic consultant: Craig Asquith

CONTENTS

2-3	The British Isles	14-15	North West England
4-5	South West England	16-17	North East England
6-7	South East England	18-19	Southern Scotland
8-9	East of England	20-21	Northern Scotland
10-11	The Midlands	22-23	Ireland
12-13	Wales	24-25	Picture quiz and Index

THE BRITISH ISLES

There are two countries in the British Isles:
the United Kingdom and the Republic of Ireland.

The British Isles is made up
of over 6,000 islands. The
largest is Great Britain.

The UK and Ireland
are divided into smaller
regions called counties.

These Scottish counties are
numbered on the map:

1. Renfrewshire
2. Dunbartonshire
3. City of Glasgow
4. Clackmannan
5. West Lothian
6. City of Edinburgh
7. Midlothian
8. East Lothian
9. Berwickshire
10. Roxburgh, Ettrick and Lauderdale
11. Dumfries

Shetland Islands

Shetland

North Sea

Orkney Islands

Orkney

SCOTLAND

Caithness

Sutherland

Ross and Cromarty

Inverness

Nairn

Moray

Banffshire

Aberdeenshire

City of Aberdeen

Kincardineshire

Angus

City of Dundee

Perth and Kinross

Fife

Stirling and Falkirk

EDINBURGH

4

5 6 7 8

Tweedale

10

9

Lanarkshire

11

Argyll and Bute

Ayrshire and Arran

2

3

1

Northumberland

Outer Hebrides

Inner Hebrides

Western Isles

Derry/ Londonderry

Donegal

Ireland is made up of Northern
Ireland, which is part of the UK,
and the Republic of Ireland.

Atlantic Ocean

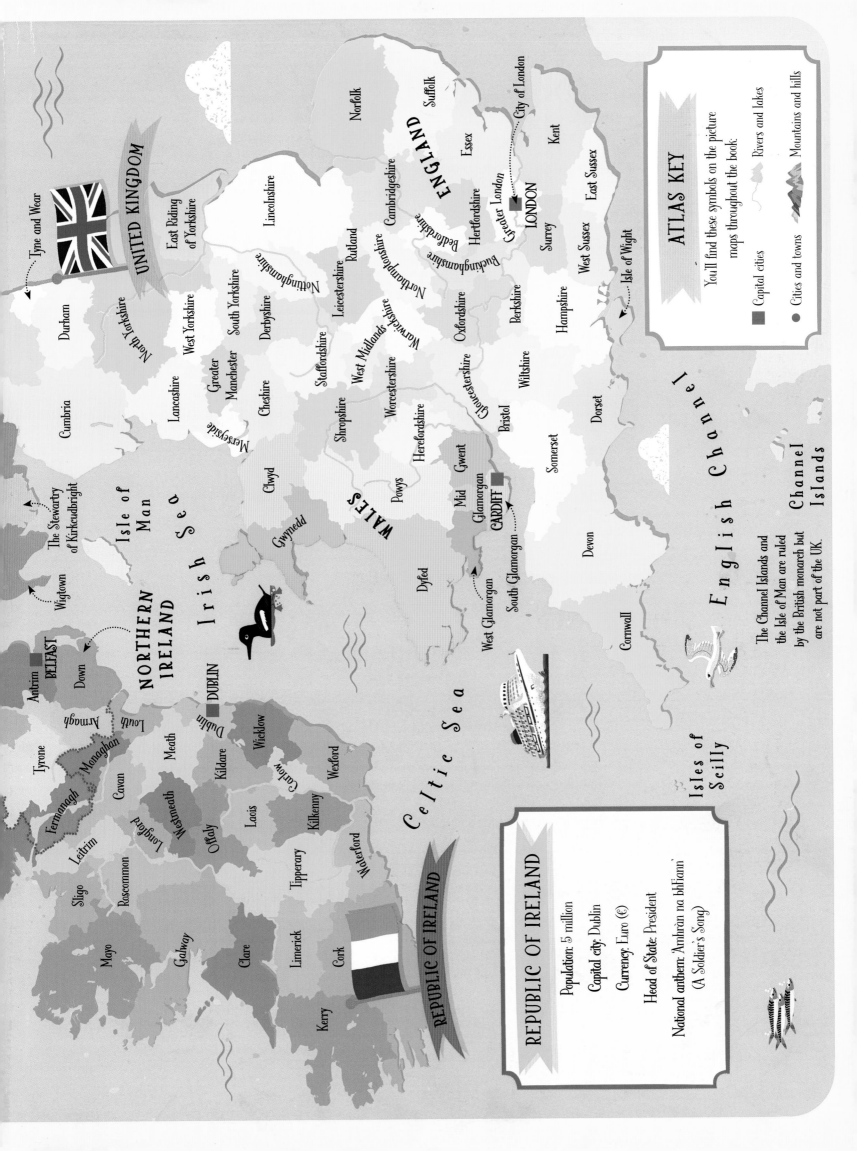

UNITED KINGDOM

Tyne and Wear

Durham

Cumbria

North Yorkshire

East Riding of Yorkshire

West Yorkshire

Lancashire

Greater Manchester

Cheshire

South Yorkshire

Derbyshire

Nottinghamshire

Lincolnshire

Merseyside

Norfolk

Suffolk

ENGLAND

Staffordshire

Shropshire

West Midlands

Warwickshire

Leicestershire

Rutland

Northamptonshire

Cambridgeshire

Bedfordshire

Buckinghamshire

Hertfordshire

Essex

Herefordshire

Worcestershire

Gloucestershire

Oxfordshire

Greater London

City of London

LONDON

Surrey

Kent

West Sussex

East Sussex

Isle of Wight

Berkshire

Hampshire

Bristol

Wiltshire

Somerset

Dorset

Devon

Cornwall

WALES

Clwyd

Gwynedd

Powys

Dyfed

Gwent

Mid Glamorgan

South Glamorgan

CARDIFF

West Glamorgan

Isle of Man

The Stewartry of Kirkcudbright

Wigtown

NORTHERN IRELAND

Irish Sea

BELFAST

Antrim

Down

Armagh

Louth

Tyrone

Fermanagh

Monaghan

Cavan

Leitrim

Sligo

Mayo

Roscommon

Longford

Westmeath

Meath

DUBLIN

Dublin

Kildare

Wicklow

Carlow

Laois

Offaly

Kilkenny

Wexford

Waterford

Tipperary

Limerick

Clare

Galway

Kerry

Cork

Celtic Sea

English Channel

Channel Islands

Isles of Scilly

ATLAS KEY

You'll find these symbols on the picture maps throughout the book.

■ Capital cities

● Cities and towns

〰 Rivers and lakes

⛰ Mountains and hills

The Channel Islands and the Isle of Man are ruled by the British monarch but are not part of the UK.

REPUBLIC OF IRELAND

Population: 5 million

Capital city: Dublin

Currency: Euro (€)

Head of State: President

National anthem: 'Amhrán na bhFiann' (A Soldier's Song)

SOUTH WEST ENGLAND

Basking shark

Pilchards

Fishing boat

Herring gull

Sea urchin

John Dory fish

Jumbo, a traditional sailing boat

Surfing

Lundy

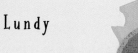
Paddle steamer

Bristol Channel

Dormouse

THE CORNISH LANGUAGE

Cornish is completely different from English. The Cornish for Cornwall is 'Kernow'.

KERNOW

Myttin da!

This means 'Good morning!'

Fatla genes?

This means 'How are you?'

According to legend, King Arthur ruled Britain with his Knights of the Round Table in the 6th century.

King Arthur and his knights

Scones with jam and clotted cream

Ruins of a tin mine

Tintagel Castle ruins

Tamar

Some historians think that Tintagel Castle has links to King Arthur.

Dartmoor pony

In the 18th century, smugglers secretly brought goods ashore in remote coves along the coast of Cornwall.

Smugglers

Truro

The Eden Project

Plymouth

The Mayflower

Exotic flowers, Tresco Abbey Garden

Isles of Scilly

St. Michael's Mount

Land's End is the most westerly point on mainland Britain.

Cornish pasty

In 1620, a group known as the Pilgrims or the Pilgrim Fathers sailed the *Mayflower* from Plymouth to America, where they founded one of the first European settlements.

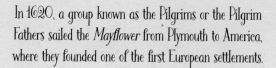

Regency townhouse

Regency-style houses were built as grand residences for wealthy people in the early 19th century.

Cheltenham Gold Cup, a horse racing trophy

Severn

Cheltenham

Gloucester

Astronaut at the UK Space Agency

The SS *Great Britain* is a steam-powered ship which sailed between Bristol and New York in the 19th century.

Cheese rolling race, Cooper's Hill

Swindon

White horse hill figure

SS *Great Britain* museum

Bristol

Roman baths, Bath

Bath

There are many hill figures in Wiltshire. They are made by scraping away grass and soil to show the white stone underneath.

Wookey Hole cave

Trowbridge

Stonehenge

Apples for making cider

Cottages on Gold Hill, Shaftesbury

Salisbury

Stonehenge is a stone monument over 4,000 years old.

Taunton

Glastonbury music festival

Tank Museum, Bovington

Beach deckchairs

Jurassic Coast fossils

Exe

Lace museum, Honiton

Exeter

Poole

Dorchester

Bournemouth

Ice cream

Fossils hundreds of millions of years old are preserved in rock along the Jurassic Coast

Bucket and spade

Durdle Door rock formation

English Channel

The Spanish Armada

The area shown on these pages is marked in red on this map.

In 1588, Spain attacked England with a huge fleet of ships called the Spanish Armada. The English navy defeated it and then chased the remaining Spanish ships through the English Channel.

Police boat

SOUTH EAST ENGLAND

British Prime Minister Winston Churchill (lived 1874-1965) was born at Blenheim Palace.

Blenheim Palace

River Great Ouse

Milton Keynes

Enigma, a coding machine at Bletchley Park

In the Second World War, British codebreakers worked at Bletchley Park to decipher enemy messages.

Oxford University students

Oxford

Traditional cottages in The Cotswolds

Rowing race, Henley Regatta

High Wycombe

Slough

Playing polo

Reading

Ladies' Day at Ascot Racecourse

Woking

Hampshire hog

Basingstoke

Jane Austen (1775-1817), an author

Red Arrows aerobatics display at Farnborough air show

THE ROYAL NAVY

Britain's Royal Navy was once the most powerful in the world. Portsmouth's Historic Dockyard is home to many ships and museums celebrating its rich history.

The *Mary Rose*, a Tudor warship from the 16th century

HMS *Victory*, Horatio Nelson's ship at the Battle of Trafalgar (1805)

HMS *M.33*, a battleship from the First World War

Winchester College is one of the oldest schools in the world. It was founded in 1382.

Test

Winchester College

Southampton

Portsmouth Historic Dockyard

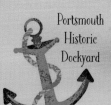

Burnt orchid flowers, South Downs

New Forest pony

Portsmouth

The Needles

Glass-blowing

Sailing race during Cowes Week

Isle of Wight

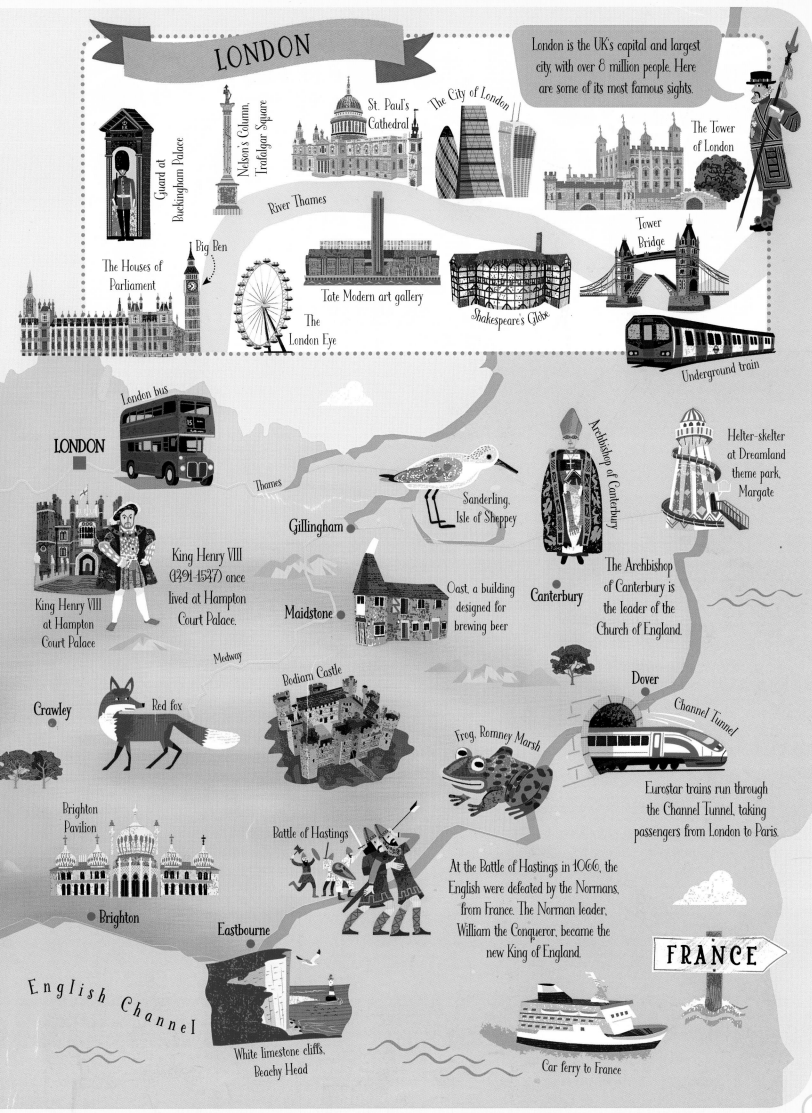

LONDON

London is the UK's capital and largest city, with over 8 million people. Here are some of its most famous sights.

Guard at Buckingham Palace

Nelson's Column, Trafalgar Square

St. Paul's Cathedral

The City of London

The Tower of London

River Thames

Big Ben

The Houses of Parliament

The London Eye

Tate Modern art gallery

Shakespeare's Globe

Tower Bridge

Underground train

LONDON

London bus

Thames

Sanderling, Isle of Sheppey

Archbishop of Canterbury

Helter-skelter at Dreamland theme park, Margate

Gillingham

King Henry VIII (1491-1547) once lived at Hampton Court Palace.

King Henry VIII at Hampton Court Palace

Oast, a building designed for brewing beer

Maidstone

Canterbury

The Archbishop of Canterbury is the leader of the Church of England.

Medway

Dover

Bodiam Castle

Crawley

Red fox

Frog, Romney Marsh

Channel Tunnel

Eurostar trains run through the Channel Tunnel, taking passengers from London to Paris.

Brighton Pavilion

Battle of Hastings

At the Battle of Hastings in 1066, the English were defeated by the Normans, from France. The Norman leader, William the Conqueror, became the new King of England.

Brighton

Eastbourne

FRANCE

English Channel

White limestone cliffs, Beachy Head

Car ferry to France

EAST OF ENGLAND

Offshore wind farm

Thornback ray

Crab

Samphire, a sea vegetable

Horatio Nelson was born in north Norfolk in 1758. He became Vice Admiral of the Royal Navy and defeated the French leader Napoleon at the Battle of Trafalgar in 1805.

Horatio Nelson

BeWILDerwood forest adventure park

Sailing, Norfolk Broads

The Norfolk Broads

Bittern

Waveney

The Norfolk Broads is an area of rivers, lakes and wetlands.

Norwich

Land yachting

K01

Sandringham House

Norwich market

Norfolk terrier

Ely Cathedral

Thetford Forest

The Royal Family often spends holidays at this country retreat.

King's Lynn

River Great Ouse

Skylark

The Wash

King John losing the Crown Jewels

In 1216, King John was on the way to King's Lynn, when the tide came in. His cart was trapped and swept into the Wash, with the Crown Jewels inside.

Water vole

Wicken Fen windpump

Show jumping

Peterborough

Oliver Cromwell

Oliver Cromwell was a political leader who defeated King Charles I in the English Civil War (1642-1651).

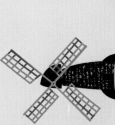

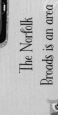

North Sea

Beach huts, Southwold

Anglo-Saxon helmet

7th-century Anglo-Saxon helmet found at Sutton Hoo archaeological site

Cruise ship

Ipswich

Roman soldier

Stour

Ickworth House

Traditional cottage, Lavenham

Colchester

Colchester was once the capital of Roman Britain.

The Thames Estuary

Southend Pleasure Pier

John Constable

John Constable (1776–1837) painted Suffolk's picturesque landscapes.

Bluebells

Southend-on-Sea

Grafham Water

Saffron Walden maze

Chelmsford

Basildon

Goods bound for London arrive at the Port of Tilbury.

Tilbury docks

Cambridge

Imperial War Museum, Duxford

Epping Forest

Camping in Epping Forest

Cambridge University

Lavender farm, Hitchin

Bedford

Woburn Safari Park

Hatfield House

Luton

Hemel Hempstead

Watford

EPPING FOREST

Here is some of the wildlife you can see in Epping Forest

Soprano bat

Great crested newt

Grey squirrel

Yellow clouded butterfly

THE MIDLANDS

Peak District

Chatsworth House

Buxton is a spa town famous for the quality of its fresh mineral water.

Buxton

Chesterfield

Water fountain, Buxton

Bakewell pudding

Pottery kiln

Stoke-on-Trent

Wedgwood china

Alton Towers theme park

Derby

Silver-studded blue butterflies at Prees Heath Common

Shrewsbury

Iron Bridge

Built in 1781, the Iron Bridge was the first bridge in the world to be made from cast iron.

Locksmith's House museum

Wolverhampton

Birmingham

Library of Birmingham

Coventry

Severn

Warwick Castle

WALES

Medieval fair at Ludlow Castle

Cricket

Worcester

Stratford-upon-Avon

Hereford cattle

Hereford

International Centre for Birds of Prey

Worcestershire sauce

A performance by the Royal Shakespeare Company

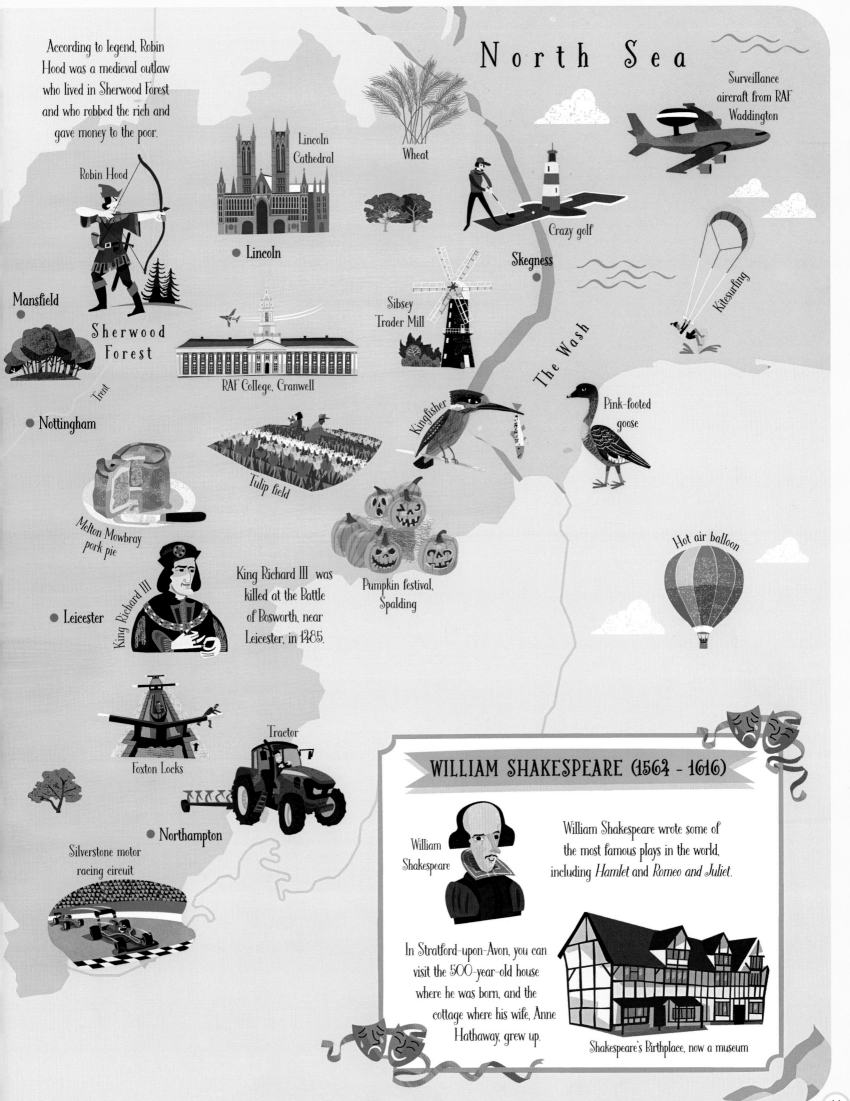

According to legend, Robin Hood was a medieval outlaw who lived in Sherwood Forest and who robbed the rich and gave money to the poor.

North Sea

Surveillance aircraft from RAF Waddington

Wheat

Lincoln Cathedral

Robin Hood

Crazy golf

Lincoln

Skegness

Mansfield

Sherwood Forest

Kitesurfing

Trent

Sibsey Trader Mill

RAF College, Cranwell

The Wash

Nottingham

Kingfisher

Pink-footed goose

Tulip field

Melton Mowbray pork pie

Hot air balloon

King Richard III

King Richard III was killed at the Battle of Bosworth, near Leicester, in 1485.

Pumpkin festival, Spalding

Leicester

Tractor

Foxton Locks

Northampton

Silverstone motor racing circuit

WILLIAM SHAKESPEARE (1564 - 1616)

William Shakespeare

William Shakespeare wrote some of the most famous plays in the world, including *Hamlet* and *Romeo and Juliet*.

In Stratford-upon-Avon, you can visit the 500-year-old house where he was born, and the cottage where his wife, Anne Hathaway, grew up.

Shakespeare's Birthplace, now a museum

WALES

ENGLAND

Irish Sea

Owain Glyndŵr was a Welsh prince who fought bravely, but unsuccessfully, against English invaders in the 1200s.

Owain Glyndŵr

Wrexham

Dee

Rhyl

Pontcysyllte Aqueduct

Offa's Dyke is an ancient earthwork. It was built by King Offa in around 780, to defend his kingdom from attacks.

Offa's Dyke

Welsh cakes

Colwyn Bay

Conwy Castle

Llandudno seaside pier

At 1,086m (3,560ft), Mount Snowdon is the highest mountain in Wales.

Mount Snowdon

Snowdonia

Pistyll Rhaeadr waterfall

Mountains

Talyllyn Railway

Aberystwyth

Puffin

Isle of Anglesey

LLANFAIRPWLLGWYNGYLLGOGERYCHWYRNDROBWLLLLANTYSILIOGOGOGOCH

This is the name of a town on Anglesey. It is the longest place name in Europe.

Menai Strait

Caernarfon

Portmeirion china set

Welsh doll in traditional costume

Cardigan Bay

South Stack Lighthouse

Hawk fighter plane

Caernarfon Bay

Merlin

Bardsey Island

Porpoise

Merlin, the wizard from legends about King Arthur, is said to have lived on Bardsey Island.

Wildlife-watching trip

Laverbread is a paste made from cooked seaweed.

Fried breakfast with laverbread

Lobster

Teifi

Fishguard

Harp, a national symbol

Periwinkles in a rockpool

Daffodils

St. David's

Gannet

Shipwreck diving

National Botanic Garden of Wales

Dylan Thomas (1914–1953), a poet

Carmarthen Bay

Bristol Channel

Boats in Swansea Marina

Swansea

Towy

Rugby

Mountain biking

Cambrian

Red kite

Brecon Beacons

Hay-on-Wye Book Festival

Wye

Leeks

Tintern Abbey

Newport

Severn Estuary

Blaenavon Coal Mine

St Fagans National History Museum

CARDIFF

Millennium Stadium

WELSH

Many people in Wales speak the Welsh language as well as English.

CYMRU

The Welsh for Wales is 'Cymru', pronounced 'kum-ri'.

Mae'n wych!
(pronounced 'mine woysh')

This means, 'It's fantastic!'

NORTH WEST ENGLAND

SCOTLAND

LITERATURE IN THE LAKES

The Lake District has inspired many famous writers, including William Wordsworth and Beatrix Potter.

I wandered lonely as a cloud...

William Wordsworth (1770-1850) wrote many poems about the natural beauty of the Lake District

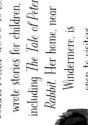

Beatrix Potter (1866-1923) wrote stories for children, including *The Tale of Peter Rabbit*. Her home, near Windermere, is open to visitors.

Army training area

Rabbit

River rafting

Eden

Caving

The Pennines

Kendal mint cake

Yorkshire Dales

Barn owl

Damson plum jam

Damson Jam

Archery

Sticky toffee pudding

Kendal

Carlisle Castle

Carlisle

Herdwick lambs

Boating on a lake

Lake District

Pencil Museum, Keswick

Scafell Pike (978m, 3,209ft)

There are 16 lakes in the Lake District. This one, Windermere, is the largest.

Hiking boots

Osprey

Solway Firth

Cumberland sausage

Black guillemot

Shortfin mako shark

Search and rescue helicopter

Red rose, a symbol of Lancashire

Lancaster

Barrow-in-Furness

Jellyfish

Wild boar in the Forest of Bowland

Laneashire hot pot, a type of stew

Blackpool Tower

Blackpool

Victorian carousel, Southport

Truck at the Commercial Vehicle Museum, Leyland

Blackburn

Birdwatching at Martin Mere

Rochdale

National Football Museum

Bolton

Wigan

Barge on Bridgewater Canal

Salford

Manchester

Sale

Stockport

Macclesfield

Quarry Bank Mill

Lovell Telescope

Little Moreton Hall, a Tudor manor house

Crewe

Weaver Workhouse Museum

Warrington

St. Helens

Liverpool

The Beatles

Birkenhead

Chester

Eastgate Clock

Hack Green Secret Nuclear Bunker

WALES

Plane from Manchester Airport

The Beatles were a pop group in the 1960s and 70s, and the best-selling band of all time.

Irish Sea

Isle of Man

Isle of Man flag

Laxey Wheel

Douglas

Motorcycle racing

Ocean liner

MUSEUM OF SCIENCE AND INDUSTRY

Here are some of the things you'll find at this famous museum in Manchester:

'Baby', a pioneering computer built in 1948

Cotton spinning machine from the 1800s

A Roe triplane, the first British plane, from 1909

The world's first railway station, which opened in 1830

NORTH EAST ENGLAND

SCOTLAND

White-beaked dolphin

Special Boat Service soldiers training

Howay!
Newcastle slang for 'Come on!'

Cod

Octopus

North Sea

Ferry to The Netherlands

Dogfish

Flock of migrating brent geese

Venus clams

Conger eel

Diving in the Great North Eastern Rocky Reef

Lifeboat on patrol

Wind turbines

Berwick-upon-Tweed

Lindisfarne Holy Island

Lindisfarne

Tweed

Coldstream Guards

Adder

Kielder Forest Park

Alnwick Castle

Cragside country house

Alnwick

Rock climbing

A fort on Hadrian's Wall

Badger

Tyne Bridge

Newcastle-upon-Tyne

Sunderland

Angel of the North sculpture

Durham Cathedral

Middlesbrough

The Pennines

High Force waterfall

Hadrian's Wall was built by the Romans around 1,900 years ago.

Tees

Minke whale

Fish and chips

Scarborough

North York Moors

Pipistrelle bat

Castle Howard

White rose, emblem of Yorkshire

The Deep aquarium

Kingston upon Hull

Grimsby

Heron

The Humber Bridge

Trent

Wild flower meadow

NATIONAL RAILWAY MUSEUM

Mallard could travel at over 200km/h (125mph).

There are nearly 300 trains on show at the National Railway Museum in York. The most famous of all is the fastest ever steam locomotive: *Mallard*.

Jorvik Viking museum

York

Liquorice Pontefract cakes

Rhubarb

Doncaster

Parkin ginger cake

Rotherham

Sheffield

Kelham Island steelmaking museum

Fountains Abbey

Ouse

Harrogate Turkish spa

Leeds

Wakefield

Yorkshire Sculpture Park

Bradford

Huddersfield

Wensleydale cheese

Brimham Rocks

Yorkshire Dales

White Scar Cave

Brontë Parsonage Museum

Charlotte, Emily and Anne Brontë were sisters who wrote famous books in the 19th century.

Eureka! National Children's Museum

Visitors to this science museum can explore giant models of human body parts.

Roast dinner with Yorkshire puddings

Atlantic Ocean

Sea eagle

Bowl of oat porridge

Cruachan hydroelectric power station

Iona Abbey

Oban

Mull

Kayaking on Loch Awe

Corryvreckan whirlpool

Inner Hebrides

Highland Games, Dunoon

Otter

Whisky distillery

Jura

Islay

House martin

Western Isles ferry

Arran

Sailing holiday

Oysters

Purple saxifrage, a rare flower

Firth of Clyde

Langoustine

BURNS NIGHT

Many Scots consider Robert Burns (1759-1796) their national poet. Every year on his birthday, 25th January, people gather to read his poetry and eat a traditional dish called haggis.

Fair fa' your honest, sonsie face,
Great chieftain o' the puddin'-race!

Haggis is made of sheep's heart, liver and lungs, mixed with oats, onion and spices.

Royal Navy patrol ship

Red squirrel

NORTHERN IRELAND

Stranraer

North Channel

SOUTHERN SCOTLAND

Tay

William Wallace was a knight who led the Scots against the English in the 13th century.

William Wallace

Loch Lomond

Stirling

Golf, St. Andrews

St. Andrews

North Sea

Haddock

Och aye!

Scottish slang for, 'Oh yes!'

Firth of Forth

The Forth Bridge

Glasgow Science Centre

Clyde

Glasgow

EDINBURGH

Edinburgh Castle

Falkirk Wheel

The Falkirk Wheel lifts boats from one canal to another.

Wind turbines

Marching band at Floors Castle

Tin of shortbread biscuits

Tweed

Cotton mills, New Lanark

Ayr

Jedburgh Castle Jail Museum

ENGLAND

Falconry

Dark Sky Observatory

Curling

Gemrock Museum, Creetown

Dumfries

Caerlaverock Castle

Devil's Porridge Museum

This museum was once a huge ammunition factory, built during the First World War.

Solway Firth

EDINBURGH

Edinburgh, the capital of Scotland, is a bustling city with lots to see and do.

The Royal Mile is a street running from the Castle to Holyrood Palace.

In summer, the streets are filled with performers at the Fringe Festival.

Holyrood Palace is the Queen's official residence in Scotland.

Orca

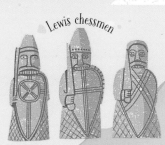

Lewis chessmen

These chess pieces were carved from walrus tusk ivory around 900 years ago.

Raven

Atlantic Ocean

Stornoway

Lewis

Hebridean ram

Spool of wool for making Harris tweed fabric

Harris

Thistle

Ullapool

Highland cow

Northwest Highlands

Gannet colony, St Kilda

St. Kilda

Kelp forest

North Uist

Outer Hebrides

Skye

Dinosaur footprint, Skye

Eilean Donan Castle

'S math sin!
(pronounced 'sma shin')

Scottish Gaelic for, 'That's good!'

Ceilidh dancing

South Uist

Barra

Sea of the Hebrides

Canna

Rhum

Glenfinnan viaduct

Fort William

Ben Nevis

SCOTTISH DRESS

Traditionally, Scottish people wear clothes made from fabric woven in a criss-crossed pattern called tartan, especially on formal occasions.

Bagpipes, a wind instrument

Tartan kilt

Ghillie brogue shoes

Balmoral cap

Pouch, called a sporran

Knife tucked into sock

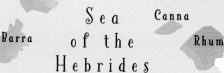

Plane

Great northern diver

Leaping salmon

Skara Brae is a prehistoric village built around 5,000 years ago.

Skara Brae

Mainland

Orkney Islands

Hoy

Arctic tern nest

Shetland Islands

Shetland pony

Yell

Unst

Mainland

Lerwick

'Up Helly Aa', a Viking fire festival

Wool sweater

Mackerel

Fair Isle

Red grouse

Red deer stag

Wick

John o'Groats is the most northerly settlement on mainland Britain.

An RAF 'Typhoon' fighter jet

Five headless ghosts are said to haunt Dunphail Castle near Inverness.

Heather

Headless ghosts, Dunphail Castle

Pictish stone from around the year 800

Lighthouse museum, Fraserburgh

North Sea

Inverness

Cairngorms

Skiing

Loch Ness

Oil rig

Aberdeen

Balmoral Castle

Scottie dog

Knight's suit at Glamis Castle

Fish smokehouse

Clay pigeon shooting

Tay

Dundee

Scone Palace

MUNRO BAGGING

In Scotland, any mountain over 912m (3,000ft) high is known as a 'munro'. The name comes from Sir Hugh Munro, a 19th-century mountaineer.

There are 282 munros in total. 'Munro baggers' are hikers who try to climb them all.

Ben Nevis is the highest munro, and the highest mountain in the UK. It is 1,345m (4,411ft).

IRELAND

SCOTLAND

Atlantic Ocean

North Channel

Irish Sea

C.S. Lewis

TITANIC

BELFAST
The *Titanic* Museum

The ship *Titanic* was built in Belfast

Giant's Causeway

A legend says that these rocks were made by a giant called Finn MacCool

Lough Neagh

Drogheda

Spoonbill

Newgrange Stone Age tomb

Erne

NORTHERN IRELAND

Derry/ Londonderry

Fanad Lighthouse

Pike fishing

Hedgehog

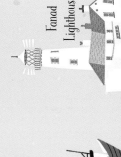
fishing boats

Hurling

Horse racing

Slieve League

These are the highest sea cliffs in Europe.

Celtic cross

Fáilte!
(pronounced 'fal-che')

This means 'Welcome!' in Irish Gaelic.

Grace O'Malley

Grace, or Gráinne, O'Malley was a terrifying pirate in the 1500s. She became known as 'The Pirate Queen'.

Potato farming

Gulliver's Travels, by Irish author Jonathan Swift

During Gulliver's adventures, he visits the land of Lilliput, where tiny people hold him captive.

DUBLIN ■

● Bray

St. George's Channel

Book of Kells

Hill of Tara

Leprechaun

Ancient kings were crowned at the Hill of Tara.

Leprechauns are mischievous fairies in Irish folk tales.

Barrow

Waterford

Soda bread

Waterford crystal

Celtic Sea

ST. PATRICK'S DAY

St. Patrick's Day parade

St. Patrick is the patron saint of Ireland. St. Patrick's Day is celebrated on 17th March every year.

REPUBLIC OF IRELAND

Gaelic football

Suir

Shannon

● Galway

Shamrock

Folk music

Blarney Castle

Kinsale fishing village

● Cork

Ferry

Limerick ●

Seafood soup

Cliffs of Moher

Irish dancers

At Blarney Castle there's a stone called the Blarney Stone. It is said that if you kiss it, you become talkative and witty.

Wild goat

Bottlenose dolphin

Grey seals, Garnish Island

PICTURE QUIZ

Test your knowledge with these ten questions about Great Britain and Ireland.
Look back through the book to find the answers, and check them below.

1. What's the name of this ancient stone monument?

2. What's this bridge in London called?

3. Who is this famous Vice Admiral from Norfolk?

4. Where was the playwright William Shakespeare born?

5. What's the Welsh for Wales?

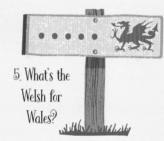

6. Which county's symbol is a red rose?

7. What's the name of the fastest ever steam train?

8. In which city would you find the Royal Mile?

9. Where is the 'Up Helly Aa' fire festival held?

10. Which famous Irish author wrote the book *Gulliver's Travels*?

Answers: 1. Stonehenge, 2. Tower Bridge, 3. Horatio Nelson, 4. Stratford-upon-Avon, 5. Cymru, 6. Lancashire, 7. Mallard, 8. Edinburgh, 9. Shetland Isles, 10. Jonathan Swift

USBORNE QUICKLINKS

For links to websites where you can take virtual tours of famous landmarks, watch video clips of wildlife and find out more about things to see and do in the British Isles, go to the Usborne Quicklinks website at www.usborne.com/quicklinks and type in the keywords **Picture Atlas Britain**. Please follow the internet safety guidelines at the Usborne Quicklinks website.

Edited by Ruth Brocklehurst   Series Designer: Stephen Moncrieff

Credits: page 17, illustration based on the sculpture 'Crawling', (1999), by Sophie Ryder © Sophie Ryder, with thanks to Yorkshire Sculpture Park.

INDEX

A
Aberdeen, 2, 21
Aberystwyth, 12
Alnwick, 16
Arran, 2, 18
Atlantic Ocean, 2-3, 18, 20, 22
Ayr, 19

B
Bardsey Island, 12
Barra, 20
Barrow-in-Furness, 15
Basildon, 9
Basingstoke, 6
Bath, 5
Beachy Head, 7
Bedford, 9
Belfast, 3, 22
Ben Nevis, 20, 21
Berwick-upon-Tweed, 16
Birkenhead, 15
Birmingham, 10
Blackburn, 15
Blackpool, 15
Bolton, 15
Bournemouth, 5
Bradford, 17
Bray, 23
Brecon Beacons, 13
Bridgewater Canal, 15
Brighton, 7
Bristol, 5
Bristol Channel, 4, 13
Buxton, 10

C
Caernarfon, 12
Caernarfon Bay, 12
Cairngorms, 21
Cambrian Mountains, 12-13
Cambridge, 9
Canna, 20
Canterbury, 7
Cardiff, 3, 13
Cardigan Bay, 12
Carlisle, 14
Carmarthen Bay, 13
Celtic Sea, 3, 23
Channel Islands, 3
Chelmsford, 9
Cheltenham, 5
Chester, 15
Chesterfield, 10
Cliffs of Moher, 23
Colchester, 9
Colwyn Bay, 12
Cork, 23
Cotswolds, 6
Coventry, 10
Cowes, 6
Crawley, 7
Crewe, 15
Cymru, 13

D
Dartmoor, 4
Derby, 10
Derry, 2, 22
Doncaster, 17
Dorchester, 5
Douglas, 15
Dover, 7
Drogheda, 22
Dublin, 3, 23
Dumfries, 2, 19
Dundee, 2, 21

E
Eastbourne, 7
Edinburgh, 2, 19
England, 2-3, 4-5, 6-7, 8-9, 10-11, 14-15, 16-17
English Channel, 3, 5, 6-7
Epping Forest, 9
Exeter, 4

F
Fair Isle, 21
Farnborough, 6
Firth of Clyde, 18
Firth of Forth, 19
Fishguard, 13
Forest of Bowland, 15
Fort William, 21

G
Galway, 23
Garnish Island, 23
Gillingham, 7
Glasgow, 19
Glastonbury, 5
Gloucester, 5
Glyndŵr, Owain, 12
Grafham Water, 9
Grimsby, 17

H
Harris, 20
Hay-on-Wye, 13
Hebrides, 2, 18, 20
Hemel Hempstead, 9
Henley, 6
Hereford, 10
High Wycombe, 6
Hitchin, 9
Huddersfield, 17
Humber Bridge, 17

I
Inverness, 21
Ipswich, 9
Ireland, 2-3, 22-23
Irish Sea, 2-3, 12, 15, 22-23
Islay, 18
Isle of Anglesey, 12
Isle of Man, 3, 15
Isle of Sheppey, 7
Isle of Wight, 3, 6
Isles of Scilly, 3, 4

J
Jura, 18
Jurassic Coast, 5

K
Kendal, 14
Kielder Forest Park, 16
King's Lynn, 8
Kingston upon Hull, 17
Kinsale, 23

L
Lake District, 14
Lancaster, 15
Lavenham, 9
Leeds, 17
Leicester, 11
Lerwick, 21
Lewis, 20
Limerick, 23
Lincoln, 11
Lindisfarne Holy Island, 16
Liverpool, 15
Llandudno, 12
Llanfairpwllgwyngyllgogery chwyrndrobwllllantysiliogogo goch, 12
Loch Awe, 18
Loch Lomond, 19
Loch Ness, 21
London, 3, 7
Londonderry, 2, 22
Lough Neagh, 23
Lundy, 4
Luton, 9

M
Macclesfield, 15
Maidstone, 7
Manchester, 15
Mansfield, 11
Margate, 7
Menai Strait, 12
Middlesbrough, 16
Milton Keynes, 6
Mount Snowdon, 12
Mull, 18
Munros, 21

N
Nelson, Horatio, 6, 8
Nelson's Column, 7
New Forest, 6
New Lanark, 19
Newcastle-upon-Tyne, 16
Newgrange, 22
Newport, 13
Norfolk Broads, 8
North Channel, 18, 22
North Sea, 2, 9, 11, 16-17, 19, 21
North York Moors, 17
Northampton, 11
Northern Ireland, 2-3, 22
Northwest Highlands, 20

Norwich, 8
Nottingham, 11

O
Oban, 18
Offa's Dyke, 12
Orkney Islands, 2, 21
Outer Hebrides, 2, 20
Oxford, 6

P
Peak District, 10
Pennines, the, 14, 16
Peterborough, 8
Plymouth, 4
Poole, 5
Portmeirion, 12
Portsmouth, 6

R
Reading, 6
Republic of Ireland, 2-3, 22-23
Rhum, 20
Rhyl, 12
Rivers
Barrow, 23
Clyde, 19
Dee, 12
Erne, 22
Exe, 4
Great Ouse, 6, 8
Medway, 7
Ouse, 17
Severn, 5, 10
Shannon, 23
Siur, 23
Stour, 9
Tamar, 4
Tay, 19, 21
Tees, 16
Teifi, 13
Test, 6
Thames, 7
Towy, 13
Trent, 17
Tweed, 16, 19
Tyne, 16
Waveney, 8
Wye, 13
Rochdale, 15
Romney Marsh, 7
Rotherham, 17

S
Sale, 15
Salford, 15
Salisbury, 5
Scarborough, 17
Scotland, 2, 18-19, 20-21, 19, 21
Sea of the Hebrides, 20
Severn Estuary, 13
Shaftesbury, 5
Sheffield, 17
Sherwood Forest, 11

Shetland Islands, 2, 21
Shrewsbury, 10
Skegness, 11
Skye, 20
Slough, 6
Snowdonia, 12
Solway Firth, 14, 19
South Downs, 6
Southampton, 6
Southend-on-Sea, 9
Southport, 15
Southwold, 9
Spalding, 11
St. Andrews, 19
St. David's, 13
St. George's Channel, 23
St. Helens, 15
St. Kilda, 20
St. Michael's Mount, 4
Stirling, 19
Stockport, 15
Stoke-on-Trent, 10
Stornoway, 20
Stranraer, 18
Stratford-upon-Avon, 10-11
Sunderland, 16
Sutton Hoo, 9
Swansea, 13
Swindon, 5

T
Taunton, 5
Thames Estuary, 9
Thetford Forest, 8
Tilbury, Port of, 9
Trowbridge, 5
Truro, 4

U
Uist, North and South, 20
Ullapool, 20

W
Wakefield, 17
Wales, 2, 3, 12-13
Wallace, William, 19
Warrington, 15
Wash, the, 8, 11
Waterford, 23
Watford, 9
Wick, 21
Wicken Fen, 8
Wigan, 15
Windermere, Lake, 14
Woking, 6
Wolverhampton, 10
Worcester, 10
Wrexham, 12

Y
York, 17
Yorkshire Dales, 14, 17